North Korea

Development, Human Rights, and Democracy

Explorations in Korean Studies

North Korea
Development, Human Rights, and Democracy

by
North Korea Modernization Research Group

IFES

KYUNGNAM UNIVERSITY PRESS

© 2010 by the Institute for Far Eastern Studies, Kyungnam University

Published by the Institute for Far Eastern Studies, Kyungnam University
Seoul, South Korea

All rights reserved. No part of this publication by be reproduced or transmitted in any form or by any means without prior permission of the publisher.

Distributed outside North and South Korea by
Lynne Rienner Publishers, Inc.
1800 30th Street, Boulder, CO 80301, USA
www.rienner.com

ISBN 978-89-8421-323-4

Contents

Introduction   1

I.   Executive Summary   7

    Modernization and Democracy   10

    Human Rights, Refugees, and Independent Media   11

    Economic Development, Participation, and Market Reform   16

    Findings and Suggestions   19

II.   North Korea's Current Challenges   23

    Politics   26

        The Workers' Party of Korea   29

        "Military-first" Politics and the Rise of the National Defense Commission   30

        The Health of Kim Jong Il, Leadership Succession, and Promotion of Family in the Leadership Structure   32

    Military   34

        The Korean People's Army and the Military-Society Relationship   35

        The Nuclear Issue   39

    Economy   40

        The North Korean Economy and Its Current Situation   41

        July 2002 Economic Adjustment Measures   43

        Domestic Economy, "Speed Battles," and Currency Revaluation   44

        Foreign Trade and Investment, the Kaesong Industrial Complex, and Kumgang Mountain Tourism   48

    Society   49

        Difficult Economic Situation   52

        Human Rights Conditions   54

        Media   56

III. The International Community's Engagement with North Korea	**59**
Modernization and Democracy	62
Changes in North Korea: A Critical View	62
Advancing Democracy through Modernization	68
Promoting Political Liberalization in North Korea: The Case of Burma	71
North Korean Human Rights, Refugees, and Media	76
Human Rights Organizations	78
Refugees	84
Independent Media	88
Economic Development, Participation, and Market Reform	91
IV. Conclusion	**95**
North Korea's Road to Modernization	97
Bibliography	**103**
The Contributors	**111**
North Korea Modernization Research Group	113
Appendix	**115**
Map of the Korean Peninsula	117
Map of North Korea	118
Index	**119**

Tables

Tables

1	DPRK government and politics	27
2	Facts on DPRK military	35
3	Main indicators of the North Korean current economic situation	42
4	Assistance of ROK government to DPRK (Unit: billion won)	42
5	Recent assistance of South Korean civilian organizations to DPRK (Unit: billion won)	43
6	North Korean society and people	50

Introduction

The issues of poverty, human rights, and democracy in North Korea (DPRK) are becoming an urgent task and a collective challenge for the international community. It is calling for harmonious efforts of both North and South Korea through reconciliation and cooperation as well as well-coordinated aid and cooperation of the international community. Therefore, it has become more urgent than ever to enhance international understanding of the major issues concerning North Korea such as development, human rights, and democracy and to build the foundation for international cooperation. Of course, in order to realize this goal, the discussions on nuclear issues and peace regime building must make progress while inter-Korean and U.S.-DPRK relations must be improved. In addition, the North Korean authorities must clearly express their intentions to the international community, to open up and reform.

North Korea is faced with a dire economic situation. In particular, securing basic living necessities for its people is a task of utmost importance. In order to help North Korea to meet this challenge, various international agencies have given humanitarian assistance to North Korea since 1995, when it called for outside help (food assistance) for the first time, and continue to do. For some donors of international humanitarian assistance, Pyongyang has been a less than stellar recipient to deal with; rather, they have found a hard authoritarian regime guided by a system of leader worship and political control to maintain public order while playing a high-stakes game of nuclear politics with the United States and its allies, among other nations. Yet other donors have managed to put politics aside, bear the complexities of the unique and at times frustrating environment, and stay the course, dealing as best as possible with the rigid bureaucracy, providing aid and assistance to the North Korean people, all the while trying to build understanding and trust—and in some cases capacity—over the long term.

Indeed, the last fifteen years have led to a polarization of the international donor community in regard to how to approach the humanitarian and economic problems of North Korea. In February 2010, in an attempt to share experience of working with the DPRK and to explore various ways of promoting

North Korea's development, human rights, and democracy through international cooperation, the Institute for Far Eastern Studies (IFES) of Kyungnam University and the National Endowment for Democracy (NED) brought together, in Seoul, numerous scholars and experts from the academic and nongovernmental organization (NGO) communities for discussion of the key issues. This monograph is one outcome of that initiative—it is both an interpretation of the presentations and discussions that took place among the conference participants and an analysis of the current situation in North Korea as seen by the North Korea Modernization Research Group of IFES.

The monograph is arranged as follows. Following a brief executive summary, section one looks at the current situation in the DPRK, drawing on a number of source materials to provide a brief description of some of the events that have recently transpired and some of the exigencies surrounding North Korea's political and military systems, economy, and society. Section two comprises the conference report, dealing specifically with the topics of modernization and democracy; North Korean human rights, refugees, and media; and economic development, participation, and market reform. Section three contains the research group's overall findings and suggestions. For further reference, the conference program, participants list, and messages from invited dignitaries and guests are included in appendices at the end.

Among the many studies and books on the situation in and cooperation with North Korea, we hope that you will find this monograph a useful resource.

I. Executive Summary

Modernization and Democracy

Human Rights, Refugees, and Independent Media

Economic Development, Participation, and Market Reform

Findings and Suggestions

A recent International Donor Conference on North Korea: Development, Human Rights, and Democracy convened by the National Endowment for Democracy (NED) and the Institute for Far Eastern Studies (IFES) of Kyungnam University brought together various concerned parties from the international donor community and nongovernmental organizations (NGOs) engaged in activities regarding humanitarian and development assistance, human rights, and democracy promotion in and related to the Democratic People's Republic of Korea (DPRK or North Korea). Participants discussed various ways to promote North Korea's development, human rights, and democracy through international cooperation. While all participants shared the same concern for the humanitarian situation in North Korea, opinions and beliefs diverged on how to approach the situation in order to create an environment supportive of positive progress in the various dimensions (i.e., political, economic, security, etc.) that would improve the overall welfare of the North Korean people in the immediate future and over the long term. Nevertheless, aspects of the North Korean issue and important dimensions discussed below for future initiatives with the DPRK deserve consideration.

Modernization and Democracy

Since the 1990s, the North Korean system has undergone vast changes characterized by "a process of desperate trial-and-error efforts for the survival of both the regime and people." Under the new system, an unstable provisional balance of power between the past and future has emerged, with the relationship between the regime and society having undergone profound transformation. The circumstances appear to have led, more recently, to a situation where social discontent is being expressed publicly, with the regime now forced to take notice and react in a manner more appeasing to the people's interests.

To advance democracy, human rights, and modernization in North Korea, closer examination of the relationship between economic development and democracy is needed. If present-day North Korea represents something roughly resembling that of South Korea during the 1960s and 1970s—as analogized—

then South Korea's "East Asian model" could stand as a viable model for the DPRK to achieve economic growth and, potentially in the long run, democracy. In simple terms, realizing democracy and human rights in North Korea may only come from a realization of the results of industrialization and a need to achieve sustainable economic growth.

Regardless of the approach, international donor organizations working to promote human rights, democracy, and development of the DPRK need to view these goals with a "long-term" mindset; in the North Korean context, results of one's aid and assistance are not always immediately apparent, in particular in terms of democracy promotion, as there is no easily identifiable democracy opposition within North Korea.

Human Rights, Refugees, and Independent Media

North Korea is generally described as one of the world's worst violators of human rights. With the number of North Koreans fleeing the country on the increase, expert focus has turned to examining the driving forces behind their decisions to leave and to explore measures that deal with solving the problem at its source. The most frequently cited motives for defection are primarily food shortages and worsening human rights and humanitarian conditions. In an effort to deal with such issues, the international community has been raising its voice to express its deep concern for the apparent escalating human rights and humanitarian violations in the DPRK. An increasing number of domestic and international nongovernmental organizations (NGOs) are working to address the issue of North Korean human rights. With more and more North Korean refugees leaving their homeland and entering South Korea, issues involving refugees or *saeteomin* (otherwise known as "new settlers") are also becoming more serious. Independent media are also making a push to gain wider attention as a legitimate vehicle for engendering change in North Korea.

The perspectives and stances regarding how best to approach the human rights situation in the DPRK and how to go about bringing actual improvements in the lives of North Koreans are manifold. Analogously, human rights organizations in South Korea and abroad differ in their values, purposes, objectives, and activities, which bring complexity to the debate. With the rise in the number of human rights organizations working both inside and outside the DPRK, specific issues have emerged as cause for concern such as the lack of outreach and coordination among nongovernmental organizations (NGOs) working in North Korea, competition for funding, a demonstrated lack of ethical guidelines and practices (especially in regard to the vulnerable groups), and credibility issues, among others. The majority acknowledge that complicated and difficult challenges exist and require concerted efforts from the various groups, especially on capacity building and training of North Korean defector-led nongovernmental organizations (NGOs). However, such efforts are inevitable and a necessary component of bringing out positive change in North Korea, for the most important resource of a nation is its people.

Over the last several years, the number of North Korean defectors who have made the perilous journey to come to South Korea has grown. If dissatisfaction among the North Korean masses intensifies, the number of defectors can be expected to grow. However, resettlement in South Korea is no bed of roses; many thorns await the "new settlers" once they arrive. Sociocultural barriers are the most formidable obstacles to their integration. The South Korean government has created work and study programs geared toward helping North Koreans integrate, and a number of churches help by providing practical information and coaching to help the new settlers cope with culture shock. Dozens of civic groups are also trying to raise awareness of or fight for North Korean defectors' rights. Several defector-led newspapers, radio channels, and associations have been set up in the past few years. The role of defectors in the future of a reunified Korea and during the process of reunification also needs to be recognized; not only are they a valuable resource for promoting integration, they can play a key role assisting North Koreans in their adjustment to a new society. Among the new settlers, the youth would become even more important, as they can play a leading role over the long run as practitioners and leaders to promote understanding, integration, and unification.

As in the past, radio stations have been a prime

source of information for people living in totalitarian and authoritarian regimes. This is also becoming the case in North Korea, as independent radio stations in South Korea begin to set up operation specifically to broadcast news into the DPRK. Participants deliberated on the role of media as a means to provide "factual" information to the North Korean populace, with some participants agreeing that "history has shown that silence has not led to progress," but rather "change has come to authoritarian countries more smoothly where independent media was most active." Currently, there are several independent radio stations based in Seoul that focus on reaching North Koreans with their broadcasts. These stations innovatively define themselves as the first independent media produced by North and South Koreans for all Koreans. A number of participants leaned toward supporting such programs run by North Korean defectors—people that the North Korean regime was said to hate and fear the most. Yet the role of such independent media in South Korea is controversial, engaging much debate, and thus a number of other participants questioned the effectiveness, motives, and ethical standards of such media organizations.

Economic Development, Participation, and Market Reform

Many would agree that stable economic growth requires democracy and that economic freedom comes from political freedom. One participant dealt with the general relationship between economic development and democracy and emphasized how this relationship is strongly interconnected. Good governance and institutions are necessary for stable economic development. Crony capitalism is not the be-all and end-all of the market system; competition and anti-monopoly policy, contract enforcement, and a level playing field for business are necessary for the market system to develop. Quality of development is equally important.

This is true even of North Korea. Today, however, the main motives behind economic policy in the DPRK are largely political, with leadership succession issues potentially having an influence in the official decision-making process, hence creating rather vacillating and confusing policy decisions.

The international community's engagement is closely tied with the lives of North Korean people in the most basic economic sense, which makes it more urgent and critical. Economic engagement with North Korea, therefore, was thought by one participant to be something promoted on two levels: short-term humanitarian aid to improve the quality of life and dignity of North Korean people, which should not be influenced by political agendas; and long-term sustainable development plans to strengthen the country's economic self-sufficiency. Improved economic self-sufficiency could more easily bring reform and openness and improvement of the human rights situation. Strategies of economic development might be directed toward improving the agriculture and energy sectors, rehabilitating social infrastructure, providing information, bolstering science and technology, and encouraging tourism.

One participant emphasized the importance of the energy sector for economic development and said that North Korea needs the help of the international community to rebuild its energy infrastructure, particularly in the electricity and coal infrastructure, as these problems feed back into the economy. Both small and large-scale improvements were identified as feasible and doable and could begin before improvements in the areas of democracy and human rights were made. International assistance for internal policy and legal reforms to stimulate and sustain energy sector rebuilding in the DPRK could involve relevant international organizations such as the International Bank for Reconstruction and Development (IBRD), the Asian Development Bank (ADB), the United Nations (UN), and applicable nongovernmental organizations (NGOs). The consequences of not developing the energy sector were seen as fatal.

Many participants agreed that economic development is necessary in order to improve the human rights situation in North Korea. Emphasis was placed on the importance of improving human rights, generally, and protecting the most fundamental rights of North Koreans. However, in order to do so, it was pointed out that humanitarian aid must be provided first. Ultimately, a move toward sustainable, self-sufficient development could be possible, as economic development is a goal shared by North Korea and the international community.

Findings and Suggestions

- The reality of working in the authoritarian DPRK means that coordination on the surface among nongovernmental organizations (NGOs) may jeopardize some of the meaningful humanitarian projects being done that actually reach the most vulnerable and intended recipients of aid. Nevertheless, the value of "networking" between nongovernmental organizations (NGOs) was recognized and could be encouraged.
- Despite the challenging environment, nongovernmental organization (NGO) efforts to expand person-to-person interaction between international society and North Koreans are desirable. More should be done to build upon the valuable work that is being done by the nongovernmental organization (NGO) community to draw out North Korea to engage in capacity-building and training at the grassroots, especially of experts in the fields of agriculture, economy, energy, and health care.
- Efforts should be made and conditions set up to encourage North Korea to pursue the road to

modernization. In this regard, the experience of South Korea in the 1960s and 1970s should be more closely examined.
- Humanitarian aid must be provided first; development that is self-sufficient and sustainable could later be made possible, as economic development is a goal shared by the DPRK and the international community.
- Political liberalization in the DPRK should be seen as a long-term goal.
- The North Korean defector community in South Korea is a valuable, growing resource. Its capacities to play a significant role in helping other defectors integrate and in the overall, long-term unification process need to be nurtured.
- International donors must be more cautious and examine more closely the local context in which potential recipient nongovernmental organizations (NGOs) operate, as the agenda and track record of some nongovernmental organizations (NGOs) are suspect and poor, while others have demonstrated a serious lack of ethical standards. Efforts must be made to equip North Korean human rights nongovernmental organizations

(NGOs) with the capacity to operate clear missions and objectives with transparent operational guidelines and codes of conduct. Donor organizations should be mindful of a potential recipient organization's abilities in these regards before providing funding.
• The capacities of independent media in South Korea, in particular radio stations, should be more closely evaluated so that they can play a constructive role in bringing positive, peaceful transformation from within the DPRK.

This report was prepared by the North Korea Modernization Research Group of IFES following the conference and workshop of February 4–5, 2010. It contains interpretations of the conference and workshop proceedings and is not merely a descriptive, chronological account of the events. It also includes a descriptive assessment of the current situation in the DPRK. Participants neither reviewed nor approved the report, and therefore it should not be assumed that every participant subscribes to the observations, evaluation, and findings.

II. North Korea's Current Challenges

Politics

　　The Workers' Party of Korea

　　"Military-first" Politics and the Rise of the National Defense Commission

　　The Health of Kim Jong Il, Leadership Succession, and Promotion of Family in the Leadership Structure

Military

　　The Korean People's Army and the Military-Society Relationship

　　The Nuclear Issue

Economy

　　The North Korean Economy and Its Current Situation

　　July 2002 Economic Adjustment Measures

　　Domestic Economy, "Speed Battles," and Currency Revaluation

　　Foreign Trade and Investment, the Kaesong Industrial Complex, and Kumgang Mountain Tourism

Society

　　Difficult Economic Situation

　　Human Rights Conditions

　　Media

The last two decades have been turbulent ones for the DPRK, with many of its citizens having suffered economic privation and extreme political oppression. While defectors' testimonies, media investigations, first hand accounts of nongovernmental organization (NGO) personnel, uncovered documents, hidden videos, satellite imagery, and various other sources and technologies have augmented our collage of evidence on this reclusive country and the plight of its people, our understanding of North Korea and its society remains deficient. However, with what we do know, some definite assumptions can be made: the country's infrastructure continues to erode and its economy remains in dire straits, its future bleak; the years of austerity and deprivation have led to a situation where the relationship between the people and the ruling regime has changed significantly; the reality of human rights in the country remains dreadful, despite North Korean human rights–related legislation and UN resolutions that have been adopted by various governments around the world to pressure the leadership in Pyongyang to make amends; the DPRK leader Kim Jong Il remains firmly at the helm of power despite his deteriorating health and has overseen the rise of the military's influence in affairs of the state and society; the political apparatus appears readying for a transformation of sorts, as the system prepares for leadership succession. This section provides some general information on the North Korean system, its society, and recent events in order to provide the reader with some rough background on the reality and issues that informed conference participants prior to their discussions. While no examination can claim to be completely objective—with observers' and experts' views on some aspects of the DPRK diverging widely, as was made manifest at our conference itself—this section provides for the reader some general facts and assessment of the country, including words from the DPRK media that illustrate the North Korean worldview.

Politics

The WPK is the most mature and sophisticated staff of the revolution in our era, and it is the great motherly party that brings valuable life and endless happiness to our people.

We should have the slogan, "If the party decides, we will do!" become the eternal motto of our people's life and struggle.[1]

— 2010 New Year's Joint Editorial

Table 1. DPRK government and politics

Country name: English - Democratic People's Republic of Korea (DPRK; North Korea); Korean - Chosun-minjujuui-inmin-konghwaguk (Choson)

Government type: Communist state, one-man dictatorship

Capital: Pyongyang

Administrative divisions: 9 provinces (*do*) - Chagang-do (Chagang), Hamgyong-bukto (North Hamgyong), Hamgyong-namdo (South Hamgyong), Hwanghae-bukto (North Hwanghae), Hwanghae-namdo (South Hwanghae), Kangwon-do (Kangwon), Pyongan-bukto (North Pyongan), Pyongan-namdo (South Pyongan), Yanggang-do (Yanggang); 2 municipalities (*si*) - Nason-si, Pyongyang-si

Independence: August 15, 1945 (from Japan)

Constitution: adopted 1948; revised in 1972, 1992, 1998, 2009

Legal system: based on Prussian civil law system with Japanese influences and Communist legal theory; no judicial review of legislative acts; has not accepted compulsory ICJ jurisdiction

Suffrage: 17 years of age; universal

---

1. "North Korea's 2010 New Year's Joint Editorial" (English translation), posted on Northeast Asian Matters, January 1, 2010, retrieved February 10, 2010, from http://asiamatters.blogspot.com/2010/01/north-koreas-2010-new-years-joint.html.

Executive branch:

> chief of state – Kim Jong Il (since July 1994); note: on April 9, 2009, rubberstamp Supreme People's Assembly (SPA) reelected Kim Jong Il chairman of the National Defense Commission, a position accorded the nation's "highest administrative authority"; SPA reelected Kim Yong Nam in 2009 president of its Presidium also with responsibility of representing the state and receiving diplomatic credentials
>
> head of government – Premier Kim Yong Il (since April 11, 2007)
>
> cabinet – Naegak (cabinet) members, except for Minister of People's Armed Forces, are appointed by the SPA
>
> elections – last election held September 2003
>
> election results – Kim Jong Il and Kim Yong Nam were the only nominees and ran unopposed

Legislative branch: unicameral Supreme People's Assembly (Choego Inmin Hoeui) has 687 seats, with members elected by popular vote to serve a five-year term; elections were held last March 8, 2009

Judicial branch: Central Court, with judges elected by the SPA

Political parties [leaders]: major party - Korean Workers' Party (KWP) [Kim Jong Il]; minor parties - Chondoist Chongu Party [Ryu Mi Yong], Social Democratic Party [Kim Yong Dae]; note: both minor parties are under the control of the KWP

Political pressure groups and leaders: none

International organization participation: ARF, FAO, G-77, ICAO, ICRM, IFAD, IFRCS, IHO, IMO, IOC, IPU, ISO, ITSO, ITO, NAM, UN, UNCTAD, UNESCO, UNIDO, UNWTO, UPU, WFTU, WHO, WIPO, WMO

Source: Central Intelligence Agency (CIA), *The World Factbook*, retrieved March 2010 from https://www.cia.gov/library/publications/the-world-factbook/geos/kn.html#.

The Workers' Party of Korea

The North Korean political system is characterized by autocracy, with a single-party dictatorship by the Workers' Party of Korea (WPK). The government severely limits freedom of expression and keeps close surveillance on the activities of the country's citizens. Since the birth of the DPRK in 1948, the party has held superiority over the state and the political management of the country has been highly personalized around the leader (formerly Kim Il Sung, and currently his son, Kim Jong Il).

As stipulated in the DPRK Socialist Constitution, the country "shall carry out all activities under the leadership of the Workers' Party of Korea," which itself is both a "class party" and one controlled by "the sole leader." With 18 departments—streamlined from 21 as of 2010—the WPK is the highest organ of power. Its supreme guiding organ is the General Assembly, which is technically held every five years, with the Party Central Committee performing the party's roles between the regular sessions of the assembly.

"Military-first" Politics and the Rise of the National Defense Commission

While the WPK is the central organ in the political power structure, Kim Jong Il has ruled the country in his position as the chairman of the National Defense Commission (NDC) since his father's death. Prior to the 1998 constitutional amendments, the National Defense Commission was a mere departmental subcommittee of the Central People's Committee. The amendments brought about an expansion of the NDC in size and authority and made it the second most important state organization, after the Supreme People's Assembly (SPA), with the NDC chairman overseeing all matters of the state.[2]

Amendments to the constitution in 1998 not only reinforced the importance of Kim Il Sung's long-

---

2. While some North Korea watchers may contend that the NDC is the "supreme power organ," Kim Jong Il supposedly does not preside over the NDC meetings, which suggests that these meetings are not for policy consultation but rather for policy implementation. Seong-Chang Cheong, "Kim Jong Il's Military-First Politics and a Change in the Power Elite," in Haksoon Paik and Seong-Chang Cheong, eds., *North Korea in Distress* (Seoul: The Sejong Institute, 2008), p. 34.

standing ruling ideology, *juche* ("self-reliance"), but also introduced Chairman Kim Jong Il's now trademark *songun* ("military-first") politics, which essentially articulate the enhanced role of the military in state affairs.

Recent restructuring of the party and amendments to the constitution in April 2009 seem to have further strengthened the supremacy of Kim Jong Il, as the chairman of the NDC was formally made the "supreme leader" of the DPRK, overseeing "the entire national business."

Likewise, the authority of the NDC was articulated as the "supreme governing authority." The military's authority was bolstered in key policy-making issue areas (including operational control of the military and external liaisons),[3] and the role of "military-first politics" was formalized as a guiding principle of the state (as references to "communism" in the constitution were replaced with "*songun*").[4] As well, since April 2009,

---

3. "North's Military Strengthens Its Grip," *JoongAng Ilbo*, April 21, 2009.
4. "N. Korean Parliament Boosts Kim Jong-il's Powers," *Chosun Ilbo*, September 25, 2009.

the NDC has expanded to include new representatives from public security bureaus and supposedly many of Kim Jong Il's friends and family members such as Kim's brother-in-law, Jang Song Thaek.

Indeed, the military is playing a more central role in the country's political system. The public activities of Kim Jong Il focus largely on "on-the-spot guidance" of military-related events and installations. All facets of society are encouraged (and must follow) the "revolutionary military spirit," adopting military methods.

Kim Jong Il's Health, Leadership Succession, and Promotion of Family in the Leadership Structure

Most observers of North Korea seem to agree that the issue of leadership succession has become a major concern in Pyongyang, as Kim Jong Il's health took a turn for the worst back in 2008, allegedly suffering a stroke in the spring of that year.

If anything, the most recent constitutional amendments and party restructuring[5] do suggest the seat of power from which Kim Jong Il's successor would rule would be the chairmanship of the NDC and military-first politics. Many observers believe Kim's third son, Kim Jong Un, is the most likely to succeed him.[6] The 27-year-old Kim is reported to have been educated at the International School of Berne and has recently (as of 2009) taken a low-ranking post in the NDC.

Alongside Kim Jong Un's apparent elevation in power, Kim Jong Il's sister, Kim Kyong Hui, seems to be wielding more power within the party, as she now heads the organ in the WPK that oversees light industries,[7] one sector that received considerable attention in North Korea's 2010 New Year's joint editorial: "Light industry and agriculture are the main fronts of the struggle for improving the people's living standards."[8] The annual DPRK power structure diagram recently released by the South Korean Ministry of Unification indicates that Kim Kyong Hui is regaining power in

---

5. "Pyongyang Enacts Major Changes in Power Structure," *JoongAng Ilbo*, February 10, 2010.
6. IFES, *NK Brief*, No. 10-3-3-1, March 3, 2010.
7. "Pyongyang Enacts Major Changes in Power Structure; Kim Jong Il's Sister Powers Up In North Korea," *Sydney Morning Herald*, February 18, 2010; see also North Korean Leadership Watch at http://nkleadershipwatch.wordpress.com.
8. "North Korea's 2010 New Year's Joint Editorial."

Pyongyang since her absence from leadership for the last six years. She has also accompanied Kim Jong Il on several on-site inspections since 2009 and has even met foreign dignitaries as of late.[9] She is the wife of Jang Song Thaek, who is a member of the National Defense Commission and director of the powerful Organization and Guidance Department of the WPK, and who is said to have had taken interim control of the North Korean government in 2008 when Chairman Kim Jong Il suffered a stroke.

Military

> *The people's army is the main force of the juche revolution and the first standard-bearer in building a powerful state. The victory of the great upswing and the happiness of the people are guaranteed by the mighty military-first gun barrel.*[10]
> — 2010 New Year's Joint Editorial

---

9. "Look at Little Sister," posted on North Korean Leadership Watch, September 24, 2009; "Mr. Jang and Mrs. Kim Go Global," North Korean Leadership Watch, February 11, 2010.
10. "North Korea's 2010 New Year's Joint Editorial."

Table 2. Facts on DPRK military

Military branches: North Korean People's Army; Ground Forces, Navy, Air Force; civil security forces (2005)

Military service age and obligation: 17 years of age (2004)*

Manpower available for military service: males age 16–49 = 6,225, 747; females age 16–49 = 6,188,270 (2008 est.)

Manpower fit for military service: males age 16–49 = 4,104,964; females age 16–49 = 4,492,374 (2009 est.)

Military expenditures: N/A

Source: Central Intelligence Agency (CIA), *The World Factbook*.
* While military service is an obligation, it is technically "voluntary."

The Korean People's Army and the Military-Society Relationship

At over 1 million men strong, the North Korean military is approximately twice the size of South Korea's. According to the government, "the army is the people, the state and the party." This statement reflects just how central the army is to the country and its 23.5 million people on a daily basis. In fact, military-first (*songun*) politics and the increasing role of the military in society could be conceived as a description of how the economy works, and how the army serves as a model of social discipline and an instrument of social control. "North Korea's military is by far the largest, most capable and most efficient organization in North Korea, and Kim Jong Il is making maximum use of it."[11] Thus soldiers are engaged in such areas as agricultural production, canal digging, and power plant construction. Officers of the Korean People's Army are expected to "hold the slogan 'Let us help the people!' and solidify like steel the unity between the army and the people, which is the root of military-first Korea, and . . . set examples in society in all aspects, including ideological, spiritual, moral, sports, and artistic aspects."[12] They also guard the country's 3,000 cooperative farms, protecting harvests.

---

11. "In North Korea, the Military Now Issues Economic Orders," *Washington Post*, November 3, 2009. Another perspective would suggest that with the emphasis on *songun* also comes a change in ideology, which, alongside the underlying goal of building a powerful and prosperous state (*kangsong taeguk*), is justified by flexible and creative interpretations of the long-standing ruling ideology of *juche*. The *songun* concept replaces the proletariat and the vanguard Communist Party with the army as the driving force in society, which could be considered a significant innovation as the army is typically a less ideological and more pragmatic institution than the party. Alexander V. Vorontsov, "North Korea's Military-First Policy: A Curse or a Blessing?" Brookings Institution. May 26, 2006. Retrieved from http://www.brookings.edu/opinions/2006/0526northkorea_vorontsov.aspx.
12. "North Korea's 2010 New Year's Joint Editorial."

From one perspective, greater military involvement can have positive effects on society under certain conditions.[13] The implementation of *songun* in the mid-1990s increased the role of the Korean People's Army (KPA) in daily life. The army began to participate even more in social and economic decision making, from large-scale infrastructure development to providing its own food. While military personnel are required to serve for ten years, they spend most of their service participating in different areas of the country's socioeconomic life, thus partially serving as a resource and catalyst for economic development. The North Korean military continues to be involved in various spheres of economic activity, including infrastructure construction in the energy sector, foreign economic ties, and trade operations. If recent trends persist, the army very likely will play a significant role in the ongoing process of modernization and economic development, including privatization (as it has in Vietnam's economic transformation).

Of course, increased military involvement in soci-

---

13. Vorontsov, "North Korea's Military-First Policy."

ety has not come without its problems. For example, anecdotal evidence exists of diversion of farmers' harvests and international food aid by the military for its consumption, some of which took the form of centrally directed large-scale diversion, but much more likely—particularly over the bleakest years of the mid-1990s famine—to have been smaller-scale, decentralized diversion conducted by lower-level party, administrative, and military personnel, as lower-ranking military officers and conscripts in certain regions were not protected from the food shortages.[14] Chronic malnutrition among low-level soldiers is also said to persist.[15]

It has also been reported that corruption has increased in the rural areas due to the permanent deployment of soldiers on the farms, with farm managers paying soldiers to turn a blind eye to theft of food that is later sold in private markets. This has occasionally led to disputes among groups of corrupt soldiers and, periodically, to violent altercations.

---

14. See Stephan Haggard and Marcus Noland, *Famine in North Korea* (New York: Columbia University Press, 2007), pp. 108–125; Korean Institute for National Unification, *White Paper on Human Rights in North Korea* (Seoul: KINU, 2007), pp. 193–198.
15. "In North Korea, the Military Now Issues Economic Orders."

The Nuclear Issue

Many of the potential international and nongovernmental organization (NGO) projects for development assistance in the North may require substantial progress in the six-party denuclearization talks. The DPRK military's missile and nuclear tests have been a cause for great concern of the international community. In October 2009, the North Korean government rejected South Korean president Lee Myung-bak's "Grand Bargain" —which included a security guarantee as well as economic and political incentives and international assistance in exchange for North Korea's denuclearization—and vowed to never give up its nuclear weapons. Pyongyang also stated that because U.S. hostilities were the reason for the North's nuclear program, any negotiations need to be between North Korea and the United States. The United States has stated that it is prepared to have direct, bilateral engagement with the DPRK if it will help to bring the DPRK back to the Six-Party Talks. For its part, while it has yet to return to the multilateral nuclear negotiations, reports indicate that North Korea has not abandoned its willingness to realize the goal of denuclearization of the Korean Peninsula through bilateral and multilateral dialogue.

Economy

> *Our [goal] of building an economically powerful state is ultimately aimed at epochally improving people's living standards. Only when [we] decisively raise the people's living standards can the hurrahs of socialism and the sounds of the song Arirang of great prosperity resound more highly throughout the country and can the gate to a powerful state be opened.*
>
> *Light industry and agriculture are the main fronts of the struggle for improving the people's living standards.*
>
> *Only when steel materials come out will rice and machines come out.*[16]
>
> — 2010 New Year's Joint Editorial

---

16. "North Korea's 2010 New Year's Joint Editorial."

The North Korean Economy and Its Current Situation

North Korea remains one of the most centrally planned economies in the world. Nevertheless, the collapse of Eastern bloc governments in 1991—in particular, that of its patron, the Soviet Union—forced North Korea to realign its foreign economic relations and move slowly toward economic decentralization. The state also has grudgingly undertaken economic adjustments to accommodate the bottom-up nascent market activity—although more recent actions suggest an attempt to revert to past practice. Regardless, so-called improvements have brought less than satisfactory results. Based on the main economic indicators, the DPRK is considered a poor country. Compared with the Republic of Korea (ROK or South Korea), in terms of nominal GNI, the North Korean economy is about 1/37.7 of the ROK economy (as of 2008).[17]

---

17. As of 2008, the nominal GNI of South Korea is $935 billion.

Table 3. Main indicators of the North Korean current economic situation

	Unit	2002	2003	2004	2005	2006	2007	2008
Nominal GNI	Billion US$	17.0	18.4	20.8	24.2	25.6	26.7	24.8
GNI per capita	US$	762	818	914	1,056	1,108	1,152	1,065
Economic growth rate	%	1.2	1.8	2.2	3.8	-1.1	-2.3	3.7
Export	Billion US$	0.74	0.78	1.02	1.00	0.95	0.92	1.13
Import	Billion US$	1.52	1.61	1.84	2.00	2.05	2.02	2.69

Source: Bank of Korea[18]

The current situation of South Korean assistance toward North Korea is as below.

Table 4. Recent assistance of ROK government to DPRK
(Unit: billion won)

	2006	2007	2008	August 2009
Food	39.4	150.5	–	–
Fertilizer	120	96.1	–	–
(via) International organization	13.9	33.5	19.7	1.7
NGO	13.4	21.6	24.1	3.9
Emergency relief and misc.	40.6	47.1	–	–
Total	227.3	348.8	43.8	5.6

Note: Food assistance in 2006 was a grant, while in 2007 it was credit assistance.
Source: Materials of the Ministry of Unification for the parliamentary inspection of the administration in 2009.

---

18. Information on North Korean economy appears different in the Bank of Korea and CIA (Central Intelligence Agency) World *Factbook*, respectively. In this section, information from the Bank of Korea is presented.

Table 5. Recent assistance of South Korean civilian organizations to DPRK (Unit: billion won)

	2002	2003	2004	2005	2006	2007	2008	Sep. 2009
Own source of revenue	57.6	76.6	155.8	77.9	70.9	90.9	72.5	29.6
Support from the government	6.5	8.1	10.2	12	13.3	21.6	24.1	4.3
Total	64.1	84.7	166	89.9	84.2	112.5	96.6	33.9

Source: Materials of the Ministry of Unification

July 2002 Economic Adjustment Measures

The failure of the centrally-planned economy and collapse of the public distribution system in the mid-1990s forced many North Koreans to engage in unsanctioned market activities to feed themselves. Authorities finally grudgingly responded in July 2002, implementing "economic management improvement measures" (hereinafter, the "July 1st economic measures"), which partially allowed market economic functions, raised wage levels of workers, adjusted prices of major daily commodities to the existing black market prices, and officially permitted markets to operate. The changes appeared to signal a willingness in the regime to embrace market measures. However, more recently, Pyongyang seems to have taken measures to suppress the markets—although with mixed success, with orders to crack down on markets partially being rescinded[19]—leading many observers to question the regime's motives and resolve for change.

Domestic Economy, "Speed Battles," and Currency Revaluation

While it is hard to guess with accuracy the situation of the domestic economy, one trend uncovered by satellite, media, and tourist photos is the renovations and reconstruction taking place in the capital of Pyongyang. In particular, one can see the construction of new apartments and construction to complete the long-unfinished Ryugyong Hotel, which is being done by Egyptian conglomerate Orascom—with the rationale for the latter project rather vague.[20]

In 2009 the North also reverted to its time-worn

---

19. "DPRK Reopens Markets, Authorizes Food Sales," *NK Brief*, No. 10-2-24-1, February 24, 2010.
20. The Economist, *Country Report—North Korea*, November 2009.

policy drive known as the "speed battle," which sees mass mobilization—rather than proper resource allocation and capital investment—as a means to increase productivity. From April to September 2009, and then from September to December, North Korea embarked on "150-day" and "100-day" speed battles, respectively. The effects of the campaigns have been mostly seen in the industrial and mining sectors (e.g., increased exports of coal, steel, and refined metal to China), with North Korea now appearing to be China's second largest anthracite supplier, as sales soared 111 percent in the first half of 2009.[21] In Kim Jong Il's statement of June 25, 2009, Kim affirmed, "there are only few more years left until 2012" and "this year will mark to be a very important year that will serve as a backbone to open the doors leading toward the strong and prosperous nation which will shape the next ten to twenty years." It has been speculated that one of the motives for embarking on the second of the two speed battles was to pave the way for a smooth transition for Kim Jong Un's succession by emphasizing the success of

---

21. "North Korea Battles to Up Output in 150-day Campaign," Reuters, August 20, 2009.

the campaign on his birthday.[22]

In late November 2009, North Korea somewhat surprisingly redenominated its currency. The purpose of the redenomination was said to be an attempt to guarantee the material base in preparation for the country's march toward "building a strong and prosperous nation"—the slogan that currently dominates economic policy—by the year 2012—the centenary of founding leader Kim Il Sung's birth. It was stated that the action would help to improve the lives of the people, in part by supposedly curbing inflation, which had accompanied the continual fall of the value of the currency since the July 1st economic measures. However, market systems stopped, and it became difficult to buy food and daily necessities. Reports surfaced that discontent arose among the people. While private moneylenders were significantly affected by the currency redenomination, trade with China took a hit, and thus fewer goods began to enter the market. As the market situation deteriorated, the regime reluctantly started to allow the market temporarily from January 31 this

---

22. "North Korea to Launch the New '100-day Battle,'" *NK Brief*, No. 09-15-1, September 15, 2009.

year.[23]

Speculation has it that responsibility for the situation was imputed to individual officials. Prime Minister Kim Young Il and Park Nam Gi, the head of economic policy, supposedly apologized for this situation in the general meeting of the Cabinet. According to the North Korea watchers, especially among the independent media and defectors' groups, reports of disturbances in society continued to surface, and distrust among the people against the regime seems to have increased. Nonetheless, some experts argued that these disturbances were temporary and the North Korean society is now well under control of the regime.[24]

Last January, the North Korean government announced its establishment of a national development bank, seemingly recognizing the inflow of resources from abroad as the most important variable for the success of the currency redomination.

---

23. "DPRK Reopens Markets, Authorizes Food Sales."
24. Alexander Mansourov, "North Korea: Changing but Stable," *Northeast Asia Peace and Security Network Policy Forum Online*, Nautilus Institution, May 12, 2010, retrieved from http://www.nautilus.org/fora/security/10027/Mansourov.html.

Foreign Trade and Investment, the Kaesong Industrial Complex, and Kumgang Mountain Tourism

North Korea's semi privatization of the economy and its desperate need to earn foreign exchange suggest that the country is more open to foreign business. Nevertheless, many obstacles—such as the poor infrastructure, UN sanctions, and political risk—have deterred many an investor.

The Kaesong Industrial Complex (KIC), which was set up in 2002 and remains in the first stage of development, faces challenges. As a form of Special Economic Zone (SEZ), the uncertain political atmosphere surrounding the North Korean nuclear issue and the clearly deteriorating inter-Korean relations both have the potential to create a crisis for further KIC development. But there is also significant potential for the project to grow economically in the future. The complex can provide gradually increasing economic utility for North Korea. Currently, about 120 companies operate in the KIC. By the end of 2009, the complex's output was worth almost US$30 million per month.

Unfortunately, the other well-known inter-Korean

project, the Kumgang Mountain tourism, has yet to reopen. After several rounds of talks between North and South Korea, no progress was made. North Korea warned that it would no longer honor contracts concerning the Kumgang Mountain tourism and that it would seize all ROK assets related to those tourism projects in the DPRK if South Korea did not agree to restart the tours by the end of March 2010. South Korea shut down the tours to the mountain resort following the 2008 shooting death of a South Korean tourist by a North Korean guard at the mountain and has insisted upon conducting a joint investigation of the incident and receipt of security assurances for future tourists.

Society

Our people are great people who possess the strongest spiritual strength in the world, and our cause of building a powerful state is an invincible cause that advances with [our people's] spiritual strength as a basic weapon. There is no change in our party's position of advancing while holding fast to ideological power and spiritual might, no matter how the situation may change. We should have the masses' ideological and spiritual strength be displayed to the maximum by continually strengthening ideological education work, such as juche *idea education and military-first idea education, among party members and working people.*

We should have the slogan, "If the party decides, we will do!" become the eternal motto of our people's life and struggle.[25]

— 2010 New Year's Joint Editorial

Table 6: North Korean society and people

Population: 23.9 million (UN, 2009)

Area: 122,762 sq km (47,399 sq miles)

Major language: Korean

Ethnicity: racially homogeneous; small Chinese community and a few ethnic Japanese

Major religions: traditionally Buddhist and Confucianist, some Christian and syncretic Chondogyo (Religion of the Heavenly Way)

* *note*: autonomous religious activities now almost nonexistent; government-sponsored religious groups exist to provide illusion of religious freedom

---

25. "North Korea's 2010 New Year's Joint Editorial."

Age structure: 0–14 years: 21.3% (male 2,440,439/female 2,376,557)
15–64 years: 69.4% (male 7,776,889/female 7,945,399)
65 years and over: 9.4% (male 820,504/female 1,305,557) (2009 est.)

Life expectancy: 65 years (men), 69 years (women) (UN)

Media: The press - Rodong Sinmun (Labor Daily) - organ of Korean Workers' Party; Joson Inmingun (Korean People's Army Daily); Minju Choson (Democratic Korea) - government organ; Rodongja Sinmum (Workers' Newspaper) - organ of trade union federation; The Pyongyang Times (English-language) - published in the capital; **Television and radio** - Korean Central Broadcasting Station - radio station of Korean Workers' Party; Korean Central TV - TV station of Korean Workers' Party; Mansudae TV - cultural station; Voice of Korea - state-run external service, via shortwave; **News agency** - Korean Central News Agency (KCNA)

Source: Central Intelligence Agency (CIA), *The World Factbook.*

North Korean society is recognized as one of the most isolated and closed nations in modern times. Media portrayals of North Korea often show a gloomy illustration of the lives of North Koreans. The government has complete control of the political, economic, and social realms of its society and people. In addition, severe economic hardships that began in the 1990s, stemming from series of events including natural disasters, economic mismanagement, and serious resource shortages are continuing to be a serious problem for society. Social welfare systems, such as the food rationing system, have not functioned properly for well over a decade. During the so-called arduous march period (1994–2002), North Koreans came to no longer rely on government support and became largely self-reliant in many aspects of daily life.

Difficult Economic Situation

Social welfare systems including the food rationing system have not functioned properly since the start of the continuing economic downturn in the 1990s and the living conditions for North Koreans deteriorated. North Koreans have traditionally depended on a public distribution system for almost all daily necessities, including food, clothing, and housing. However, distribution came to a halt in the mid-1990s and since then each household has had to find its daily necessities on its own. Although it seems North Korea has recently overcome the worst of the famine, the average North Korean still faces difficulties in obtaining adequate food, clothing, and housing. As a result, individuals became more proactive in making their own living to support themselves and their families, and engaging in private economic activity has become an inevitable choice—for survival. Private farming and commercial transactions became ever more common, with markets being the sole source of providing food and necessities for families. This had changed the dynamics of society and the daily lives of the people.[26]

With changes that began to emerge in the mid-1990s, changes started to take place gradually as individuals were adapting to the new realities of life. This topic is interconnected with the economic situation of the country. Debate among scholars, experts, and outside observers continues as to whether economic improvements and development must become a precondition to human rights and promotion of independent media, or other measures to bring about actual

---

26. Jeong-Ah Cho, Bo-Geun Kim, Soon-Hee Lim, Young-Ja Park, and Jae-Jean Suh, *The Everyday Lives of North Koreans* (Seoul: KINU, 2009); "North Korean Food Shortages to Grow, Crimes of Necessity on the Rise," *NK Brief*, No. 09-11-02-1, November 2, 2009; Korean Institute for National Unification, *White Paper on Human Rights in North Korea* (Seoul: KINU, 2007); Debra Liang-Fenton, "Failing to Protect: Food Shortages and Prison Camps in North Korea," *Asian Perspective*, Vol. 31, No. 2 (Summer 2007), pp. 47–74; Michael Schuman, "The Real Crisis in North Korea? Food," *Time*, October 6, 2008; "DPRK Food Prices Unstable as Lean Season Approaches," *NK Brief*, No. 10-04-28-1, April 28, 2010.

improvements in the lives of ordinary North Korean citizens.

Human Rights Conditions

North Korea has faced numerous allegations of horrendous human rights violations. According to the 2009 U.S. State Department Country Report on Human Rights, North Korea's human rights record remains deplorable. The North Korean government is charged with numerous human rights violations, such as restricting the democratic process and limiting workers' rights, as well as limiting freedom of religion, movement, speech, press, assembly, and association. It is also responsible for extrajudicial and unreasonable public executions, disappearances, arbitrary detentions, arrests of political prisoners, harsh and life-threatening prison conditions, and torture.[27]

The international community has condemned the

---

27. U.S. Department of State, *2009 Human Rights Report: DPRK—Country Reports on Human Rights Practices*, retrieved from www.state.gov/g/drl/rls/hrrpt/2009/eap/135995.htm; Korean Institute for National Unification, *White Paper on Human Rights in North Korea* (Seoul: KINU, 2007).

human rights abuses in North Korea and, as a result, has taken action against North Korea. However, actions by the UN and other human rights organizations are criticized for not bringing about any meaningful change in North Korea,[28] with some arguing that the international community was unsuccessful in improving the human rights of North Koreans.[29] The UN Special Rapporteur for Human Rights in the DPRK, Vitit Munthaborn, has never visited North Korea and DPRK authorities have not allowed any human rights organizations to enter the country since 1996. Furthermore, the North Korean government has not acknowledged these allegations to be legitimate but rather as a threat to its sovereignty.

In the international community, there is little debate that North Koreans are, indeed, faced with an abysmal human rights situation in which the regime continues to commit serious human rights abuses. Despite consensus on this fact, there are diverging views on how

---

28. John Feffer, *"Starting Where North Korea Is,"* 38 North (Washington, D.C.: U.S.-Korea Institute at SAIS, Johns Hopkins University, May 1, 2010), retrieved from http://www.38north.org/?p=529.
29. Ibid.

best to approach and resolve the issue. The question of what should come first—the protection and promotion of economic and social rights, or political and civil rights—continues to frame the debate.

Media

Despite the fact that its constitution provides freedom of speech and press, the government is in strict control of media, controlling nearly all information. There are no independent media and the government manages visits by all foreigners, especially journalists.[30] Radio and TV sets are preset to government stations and serve as propaganda tools, exalting Kim Jong Il and reporting his daily activities. Reporters Without Borders has reported North Korea to be one of the world's worst violators of freedom of the press. In its 2008 Press Freedom Index, North Korea was ranked 172 out of 173, and was referred to as one of the "inferno trio for press freedom" along with Turkmenistan and Eritrea.[31] North Korean residents who are caught lis-

---

30. U.S. Department of State, *2009 Human Rights Report: DPRK—Country Reports on Human Rights Practices*.

tening to foreign broadcasts risk serious consequences, including forced labor, imprisonment, and possibly execution.[32] Despite such tight measures of control, North Koreans are able to receive information from various Korean and other foreign DVDs and CDs that are smuggled into the country.[33]

Controversies surrounding media centers around the increasing use of independent media for the purpose of disseminating information about the outside world to North Korean residents. The debate continues on if and how such media are or can be effective in bringing actual change to the people of North Korea, and on whether or not such media should be expanded. Clearly, more research on this topic would be beneficial.

---

31. Reporters Without Borders, "Press Freedom Index 2008," retrieved from http://en.rsf.org/press-freedom-index-2008,33.html.
32. Korean Institute for National Unification, *White Paper on Human Rights in North Korea* (Seoul: KINU, 2007), pp. 33–36; also see BBC, "North Korean Country Profile," retrieved from http://news.bbc.co.uk/2/hi/country_profiles/1131421.stm#media.
33. Andrei Lankov, *North of the DMZ* (London: McFarland & Co., 2007), pp. 309–312; "North Korea Among the Worst Media on Earth," Daily NK, October 21, 2009, retrieved from http://www.dailynk.com/english/read.php?cataId=nk00100&num=5555.

The International Community's Engagement with North Korea

Modernization and Democracy
- Changes in North Korea: A Critical View
- Advancing Democracy through Modernization
- Promoting Political Liberalization in North Korea:
   The Case of Burma

North Korean Human Rights, Refugees, and Media
- Human Rights Organizations
- Refugees
- Independent Media

Economic Development, Participation, and Market Reform

III. The International Community's Engagement with North Korea

On February 4–5, 2010, the Institute for Far Eastern Studies (IFES), Kyungnam University and the National Endowment for Democracy (NED) convened a conference and workshop devoted to strengthening international cooperation in support of development, human rights, and democracy in North Korea. This section summarizes the presentations and panelist remarks at the conference and weaves in relevant observations, opinions, interpretations, comments, and general discussion points made during the workshop. Arranged systematically according to the conference sessions that were held, this section addresses the relationship between modernization and democracy in the case of North Korea; examines, via case reports, the situation of North Korean human rights and refugees and the role that independent media play in human rights and democracy promotion; and looks at the economic development side of the democracy-promotion equation, with an assessment of the possibilities for economic engagement between the international community and the DPRK.

Modernization and Democracy

Changes in North Korea: A Critical View

No one would disagree that our picture of North Korea has been one of a tightly controlled totalitarian system—one of the most closed societies in the world. Despite our information gap on the internal situation in North Korea, we do know that changes in the historical international system in the late 1980s and early 1990s exacerbated the economic exigencies the country faced, leading to a period marked by drought, famine, and virtual collapse of the economy, a period that no doubt had a profound impact on the society and on the regime-society relationship.

One conference participant characterized the situation since as "a process of desperate trial-and-error efforts for the survival of both the regime and people." The new situation that emerged was portrayed as an "unstable provisional balance of power between the past and future," with the relationship between the regime and society having undergone profound transformation. The regime's methods of penetrating and controlling the people were said to have changed and consequently new societal conditions have been established.

In the aftermath of what has been called the "arduous march" of the late 1990s, the regime was said to have reconsolidated itself and experimented with reform (2000–2004), which included economic adjustment measures of July 2002 and increased influence of Prime Minister Park Bong Ju on the decision-making process for economic policy and the personnel affairs of the Cabinet—of which the latter was noted as being quite exceptional. The results of the reforms were said to be decidedly mixed.

This reformist phase was said to have led to a backlash by conservative elements within the regime that saw the market and its expansion as a "hotbed of anti-socialist phenomena." Changes and restructuring pursued by the regime since 2005 were said to have resulted in a new system taking shape, one that now features, among others: movement away from extension of market activities and expansion of private production toward repression of the market and expansion of production by the state; income inequality due to business results to income inequality due to bureaucratic function; movement away from decentralization toward centralization; reorganization of foreign trade firms under the National Defense Commission and the Ministry of Trade; a change in the beneficiaries favoring the party gerontocracy, party and military officials, foreign trade firms run by influential agencies, party ideology, planned economy, and socialist principles.

The recent activity and developments were said to indicate that Pyongyang might be attempting to "roll back the clock" and return to some semblance of its pre-crisis traditional system of planned economy, public distribution, and tighter controls over the population. Current internal affairs of the country were also presented conceptually: a transformation from pre-1990s totalitarianism to tyranny—although this point was later disputed by a workshop panelist; a division of the national economy into seven quasi-independent sectors—in which the sector of commercial companies has stood as representative of the transitional characteristics of the North Korean economy since the 1990s; and cleavages and stratification in society, with, on the one hand, people suffering poverty and hunger, and on the other, a newly forming rich class wanting to realize Western spending habits within North Korea.

Overall, the participant took a rather grim view of the provision of aid to the country: "It is meaningless to provide aid . . . if it does not reach the lower stratum of the population." While it was stated that meaningful change could come if political forces with strong enough will and ability for reform were to emerge, the participant was less than optimistic that such a scenario would develop.

Not everyone subscribed to this view. One participant in the workshop expressed the view that, to understand the characteristics of human rights assistance to North Korea, we need to understand its society not as a "failed society" just because the regime's main focus is to maintain its current political system, and not to see it as a state that, if pressured enough, will collapse the regime; rather, while acknowledging that the government is the perpetrator of human rights violations in the country, the participant emphasized that the international community must put efforts toward policy coordination with the North Korean government. "Without negotiations with the North

Korean government, we cannot help the most vulnerable . . . So in an ironic way, we do need to deal with the North Korean government."

Another participant shared this view: "The closer you come to the decision makers in North Korea, the closer you are to having an impact." It was also argued that programs that do not jeopardize the regime would be more accepted by the regime. "Right or wrong, this is the reality we must face." The participant suggested that, like South Korea of the 1950s, 1960s and 1970s, North Korea needs continued outside assistance, economic growth, and civil society movement—implying that the latter of the three will develop if the former two conditions are present. The participant recommended that the international community provide as much assistance as possible and that North Korea commit to economic development: "Once they have this, people will begin to fight for human rights and democracy."

Likewise, another participant cautioned about how we should look at the regime in North Korea and how to promote change. In the participant's view, North Korea should be classified into three groups: the power elite, the middle-level officials including technocrats, and ordinary citizens. It was suggested that the power elite be encouraged—sometimes pressured—to change their approach; the technocrats be given the chance to experience the outside world, with those within the group who see change in the North as a positive development destined to lead the way; and the ordinary citizens made aware of the reality in the world, for a change in the mind of the common man can influence change (for the improvement of the people's lives) in the long run. On this third point, another participant pointed out that, in the testimonies of North Korean defectors who enter South Korea, many identified external issues, like war with the United States, as their own personal issues, despite the hardships that they faced internally. Realizing this, the participant suggested that efforts be made to make North Koreans aware that there is "no threat from the outside."

Another participant agreed that policy cooperation was necessary, but that the incentives did not exist for the North Korean government to make the needed (and desired) policy changes—and thus reinforcing the above view that continued assistance is necessary.

However, others deliberated whether the assistance should come more in the form of education rather than material incentives to foster economic growth.

Advancing Democracy through Modernization

Another conference participant explained ways to advance democracy in North Korea through modernization of the country. Examining the relationship between economic development through the promotion of modernization, human rights, and democracy, the participant emphasized the need for "modernization." Characterizing the present situation in North Korea as one resembling that of South Korea during the 1960s and 1970s, he suggested South Korea's "East Asian model" as a viable model available for the DPRK to achieve economic growth and, potentially in the long run, democracy.

The participant stated that one commonality among the development states that prioritized economic growth and tried to sustain that growth was that they had experienced the unintended consequences of a demand by the people for greater democracy and greater respect for human rights. In simple terms, the participant argued that realizing democracy and human rights in North Korea will only come from a realization of the results of industrialization and a need to achieve sustainable growth. Consequently, the recommendation was for the international community to focus its assistance on helping modernize the DPRK, via, among other things, a five-point development strategy for North Korea that included (1) state-led development, (2) capital accumulation, (3) human resource development, (4) technical advances, and (5) formation and expansion of markets.

Objectives of such a strategy were described to include poverty reduction, government-led development with increasing private-sector participation, improvement in labor resources, increase in foreign capital and technology via Special Economic Zones (SEZs), and system-level improvements that see simultaneous development of the economy and society. Apart from outlining the necessary conditions, principles and goals, and examples of specific strategies to achieve modernization of the DPRK, it was recommended that the international donor community pursue a step-by-step multidimensional approach to tackle seven key challenges: (1) ensure the basic right to life (i.e., humanitarian food and nutritional aid and job creation); (2) provide social services (i.e., social and human development); (3) strengthen foreign-trading capabilities and promote science and technology; (4) establish a system to encourage market oriented reform; (5) secure support for financial soundness; (6) support North Korean membership in the international community; and (7) promote human rights and democracy.

The participant emphasized that "aid must concentrate on creating an environment that encourages [the] North's active participation in its own modernization process than passive involvement. Historical evidence indicates that market economies, including democratic systems, often fail if . . . enforced from the outside. In addition, hasty expectations that North Korea will accomplish democracy and economic development through external forces must not be made. Rather, a focus on seeking practical methods to promote development and democracy will be much more effective." In implementing such a plan, the participant added that the international community take a "farmer's view" that lays emphasis on "constant effort and patience."

While some participants agreed with the modernization approach, others questioned its practicality, as many modernization projects likely require progress at the level of high politics (i.e., the Six-Party Talks), and they cautioned that it was inappropriate to push such an approach at the expense of others. "In this kind of work, no one size fits all." Thus a "common approach" centered on working with North Korean authorities and on modernization of the country was not seen as ultimately necessary: "Germany had Ostopolitik. But others did not . . . And the U.S. has had a different approach. The U.S. had different approaches in other environments." Rather, it was believed more prudent to pursue multiple, "complementary" approaches.

Promoting Political Liberalization in North Korea: The Case of Burma

Another conference participant outlined the programs of one donor organization's work in promoting political liberalization in Asia and identified its Burma-related program as unique and relevant to the North Korea context. He explained that because Burma is so repressive and activists closely monitored, the exile movement was said to provide one of the few channels by which a donor could reach the most isolated and vulnerable groups inside the country with assistance. The strength of the exile movement was said to come from the people involved and those people's connections with those inside the country. The participant stated that the exile community served as an "important conduit for information coming into and out of the country," that it provided, inter alia, "financial support for safe-houses, communication equipment, and organizing activities," along with a wealth of information about the country.

In the case of North Korea, the participant stated that the organization's North Korea–related support was concentrated in the three main areas of (1) human rights documentation and advocacy, (2) freedom of information, and (3) civic education and capacity building for defectors. Similar to the organization's Burma-related program, the participant said that the organization viewed its work in North Korea as "long term" and that it understood that its results may not be immediately apparent. One immediate difference between the two cases that was pointed out was the lack of easily identifiable democracy opposition within North Korea.

Overall, many participants at the conference agreed with the three views presented. Nevertheless, various questions and comments highlighted the discussion.

One participant cautioned that clear definitions of terminology like "democracy promotion"—in terms of the expansion of democratic space and the building of democratic institutions—were needed before such could be discussed, while another questioned why democracy promotion was necessary and under what conditions it would be justifiable.

Other participants expressed a concern that expanding human rights and democracy promotion programs in order to exploit the North Korean regime's vulnerabilities would actually enhance the military as an instrument of political decision making, which could inter alia complicate multilateral diplomacy to encourage the regime to work toward denuclearization of the Korean Peninsula. Another pointed out the need to evaluate China as a factor to promote human rights, democracy, and modernization in North Korea.

Other participants emphasized the importance of bringing North Korean issues into the mainstream of regional democratization movements and identified the lack of a regional campaign to deal with the North Korea issue. Several participants reiterated these two points and also stressed the importance of donor coordination in aid efforts.

Another participant pointed out that North Korea's own plans to modernize by 2012 (i.e., to build a "strong and prosperous state") do not envision "openness or reform." Others pointed out the need to promote the rule of law and engagement, as well as to improve North Korean capacity to absorb international assistance and the ability to develop sustainability (in particular in the area of food security) while also continuing projects like the Kaesong Industrial Complex—as a micro-model of how North Korea can accept investment.

Still others opposed the idea of any kind of development assistance that would help sustain the "undemocratic" regime in Pyongyang. "When the regime is so focused on trying to sustain itself, then the time is right for change . . . So I ask you to consider that the North Korean regime gives up power, and what effects would that have, and how we could support these efforts."

Others expressed their total opposition to any promotion of "regime collapse." One participant saw democracy promotion in the DPRK to induce regime collapse as virtually impossible at this time. Another dismissed it as lacking possibility and probability: "You cannot separate out the general population and the military and regime—they are too well unified"; the existing military command structure and economic capabilities of the ROK could not handle such a scenario; and the geopolitics of the situation (i.e., North Korea's growing dependence on China and China's interest in maintaining the status quo stability in the region) would not allow such to happen.

Others disagreed. "No one can predict change." One participant also stated the Albanian and Romanian experiences as case-in-point that change toward democracy can come sooner rather than later. The growing amount of documentation of the increasing inflow of non-state-sanctioned media into the DPRK was also stated to be an indicator that the fear level of the North Korean people was declining.

One other participant warned that the international community should begin to work now on coordinating development assistance to the DPRK: "This situation is Africa in the making. I see in Africa they have different interests and behaviors. . . . If we don't work on coordination now, it will be a disaster in the making and North Korea will be the one that suffers. So when do we decide to start coordinating?" However, he also cautioned that, at the present time, the regime in North Korea does not seem to be concerned with development assistance at all.

North Korean Human Rights, Refugees, and Media

North Korea is generally described as one of the world's worst violators of human rights. With the number of North Koreans fleeing the country on the increase, focus has turned to examining the driving forces behind their decisions to leave and to explore measures that deal with solving the problem at its source. The most frequently cited motives for defection are primarily food shortages, worsening human rights, and humanitarian conditions. In an effort to deal with such issues, the international community has been raising its voice to express its deep concern for the apparent escalating human rights and humanitarian violations in the DPRK.

An increasing number of domestic and international nongovernmental organizations (NGOs) are now said to be working in some way to address the issue of North Korean human rights. With more and more North Korean refugees leaving their homeland and entering South Korea, issues involving refugees are also becoming a more serious social issue. Independent media has also an intention of gaining wider legitimacy as a vehicle for engendering change in North Korea. In the session on North Korean human rights, such issues as human rights organizations, refugees, and media were carefully discussed, along with direction for future improvements.

Human Rights Organizations

The debate over North Korea's human rights issue has been long-standing. The international community's interest in, and involvement with, this issue has grown but the situation in North Korea is far from being resolved. North Korea claims human rights to be solely a domestic affair and dismisses any allegation of human rights violation as a scheme against the regime. Despite such claims, the international community continues to raise these issues with the North Korean leadership, with limited impact.

There are multiple perspectives and stances regarding human rights and how to go about bringing actual improvements in the lives of North Koreans. Analogously, human rights organizations in South Korea and abroad differ in their values, purposes, objectives, and activities. These various organizations concerned about North Korean human rights engage in a variety of activities including work with defectors living and hiding in China and other third countries, the publication of information of the human rights situation in North Korea, the provision of assistance to defectors living in

South Korea, the holding of conferences and meetings for international nongovernmental organizations (NGOs), and so forth. With the rise in the number of such organizations, there have emerged specific issues that have become cause for concern.

Human rights organizations working inside North Korea are faced with the dilemmas and challenges that arise from having to work under the strict controls of an oppressive government. They also suffer from a lack of outreach and work in an environment devoid of an internal civil society or pro-democracy or human rights activists. For those organizations working in South Korea, they face the difficult realities of running an nongovernmental organization (NGO)—something that has been especially challenging for defector-led nongovernmental organizations (NGOs). These organizations are in competition with other nongovernmental organizations (NGOs) in terms of securing domestic and international sources of funding. Many were said to be inexperienced in operating such an organization, with some also facing ethical dilemmas as well as simple administrative difficulties.

One participant pointed out that a number of organizations that claim to work for the improvement of North Korean human rights have actually demonstrated a lack of ethical conduct and practices (especially against the vulnerable groups), a lack of focus or specialty, and lack of experience in the simple daily operation and management of an office and organization. These shortfalls are detrimental in securing funding from international donors and negatively affect the image and reputation of the human rights nongovernmental organization (NGO) community as a whole. Some organizations were criticized for being "self-serving" (i.e., serving the interests of a founder or leader of the organization), rather than promoting the freedom of North Koreans.

A number of participants pointed out the lack of credibility of some of the nongovernmental organizations (NGOs) working in South Korea. The political and ideological divide between the various organizations was said to be damaging. Their lack of a common goal or cooperation was also seen by some as a serious drawback, with the influx of organizations now handicapping established organizations, as they all vie for the small pool of existing resources. The political and ideological divides and the way South Korean nongovernmental organizations (NGOs) pull against each other were said to be incredibly damaging.

The lack of a credible and consistent message by these organizations was also said to be problematic. "Every year we hear about oncoming famine in North Korea . . . This creates donor fatigue, and thus we need to send out clear and credible message when we do send one." While some organizations have been said to be doing great work, even these organizations, in cooperation with foreign embassies, have suffered from a lack of initial, clear messages (which in one case has led a report intended for high-level policy makers to end up being ineffective). Some organizations were also criticized for producing—and being influenced by—inaccurate information. Since North Korea is a closed and reclusive country, it becomes even more difficult to clarify and confirm what is true and what is only mere rumor. Therefore, nongovernmental organizations (NGOs) among others were recommended to focus on work based on accurate information and analysis.

Another problem mentioned by a participant was the lack of coordination among the nongovernmental organizations (NGOs) working in North Korea. Some organizations seem to agree on the value of "networking," including with international organizations like the UN; but others also pointed out that working with these organizations in North Korea may bring about stricter restrictions against them or even eviction from North Korea, and that too much coordinated overview might actually be dangerous. One participant stated, "For nongovernmental organizations (NGOs) operating inside North Korea, if North Korean authorities get even a hint that onsite nongovernmental organizations (NGOs) are coordinating and have the objective of getting politically involved, they get kicked out . . . nongovernmental organizations (NGOs) inside need their flexibility. For example, a Belgian nongovernmental organization (NGO) working with disabled people is getting results in the area of human rights . . . but they must hide behind the umbrella of the E[uropean] U[nion]."

In terms of North Korean defector-led nongovernmental organizations (NGOs) operating in South Korea, when considering that the majority of their funding comes from foreign donors, compared to the largely domestically funded South Korean nongovernmental organizations (NGOs), it is evident that North Korean defector-led nongovernmental organizations (NGOs) need to explore other funding opportunities to fully utilize their resources. However, one participant also cautioned that international donors that fund certain domestic nongovernmental organizations (NGOs), including defector-led ones, should look more closely at why these are not being funded by the South Korean public before deciding to give funding themselves.

A combination of testimonials and case study reports from human rights organizations was effective in illustrating the current challenges of nongovernmental organizations (NGOs) engaged in North Korean human rights work. The consensus that was reached was that there are complicated and difficult challenges, requiring concerted efforts from wide-ranging groups, especially on capacity building and the training of North Korean–led nongovernmental organizations (NGOs). However, such efforts are inevitable and a necessary component of bringing out positive change in North Korea, for the most important resource of a nation was said to be its people.

Refugees

Over the last several years, the number of North Korean defectors who have made the perilous journey to come to South Korea has grown. According to the ROK Unification Ministry, as of September 2009, as many as 17,000 North Korean defectors ("new settlers") were living in South Korea—three times as many as in 2004. Around 78 percent of North Korean defectors entering the South are women.[34] As information about the outside world continues to seep into the North, as food shortages continue to plague the population, and as dissatisfaction among the masses intensifies, the number of defectors can be expected to grow.

Before coming to South Korea, most were unemployed or had been laborers. Only about 70 percent attained middle or high school education. Some are "chain" migrants, following their family or relatives who defected to the South before them.[35] Defectors

---

34. "North Korean Defectors: A Big Market for Matchmakers," *Time*, February 9, 2010.
35. Sung-jin Kim, "Actual Conditions of North Korean Defectors," *Vantage Point*, Vol. 31, No. 11 (November 2008), pp. 16–19.

who reach the South must spend approximately two months at the government-sponsored resettlement center, Hanawon, located in the countryside south of Seoul. There the center's staff helps defectors to deal with the immediate socioeconomic and psychological anxiety they feel and to overcome the barriers of cultural heterogeneity. They also provide some basic training on how to find a job or earn a living. Upon completion of the program, defectors find a home with a government subsidy, normally receiving a nominal resettlement fee and a monthly check. A large majority (approximately 67 percent) end up settling in the Seoul metropolitan area.

However, resettlement in South Korea is no bed of roses; many thorns await the new settlers once they enter society. Sociocultural barriers are the most formidable obstacles to their integration. Despite the often-cited Korean "oneness" or ethnicity, many defectors who have come end up feeling like "second-class" citizens because of their origins. Making friends with South Koreans can be difficult once they learn of the defectors' origins. Most defectors living in South Korea dislike being classified as "*talbukja*" (defector from the North), "*saeteomin*" ("new settlers"), or "*ital jumin*" ("residents of the North who have departed it"). Many would prefer to be known simply as "Koreans." In a society where family background, social standing, and education are predominant factors in getting a job, finding a marriage partner, or even making friends, terms such as the above become discriminatory. This is not the case for every North Korean defector, as those defectors with relatives in South Korea may be more eager and find it easier to integrate.

One participant stressed that the biggest challenge faced by these new settlers was the education system. "The money that the average South Korean puts into educating their child . . . is something that new settlers just cannot compete with. So in a sense, access to educational programs that will help these new settlers compete is a big problem."

The South Korean government was said to have created work and study programs geared toward North Koreans, and that churches help by providing practical information and coaching to cope with culture shock. Dozens of civic groups are also trying to raise awareness or fight for North Korean defectors' rights. Several

North Korean defector-run newspapers, radio channels, and associations have been set up in the past few years. It was also said that the incumbent government has put priority on helping new settlers get opportunities to gain good and meaningful employment—instead of just being given money—as such will allow them to obtain better benefits and incentives.

It is also imperative to recognize the role of defectors in the future of reunified Korea and during the process of reunification. Not only are they a valuable resource for promoting integration, they can play a key role in providing assistance for North Koreans as they adjust to a new society. Among them, the role of North Korean youths becomes even more important, as they can play a leading role as practitioners and leaders to promote understanding, integration, and unification in the long run. One organization was identified as just that type of organization, operated by North and South Korean youths, working to help other North Korean youths adjust and succeed in their new society so that they can work in the future and play a leading role before, during, and after reunification.

Independent Media

As in the past, radio stations have been a prime source of information for people living in totalitarian and authoritarian regimes. This is one of the key lessons from the Eastern Europe experience. During Nazi occupation, the people of France listened to Radio Londres run by the DeGaulle government in exile; under Soviet regimes during the Cold War, millions of Eastern Europeans tuned in to Radio Free Europe; and during the Taliban rule, Afghans listened to the BBC. Even today, many Cubans rely on Radio Marti—which broadcasts from Miami, Florida and is sponsored by the U.S. government—for credible news about the world. This is also becoming the case in North Korea—one of the most closed societies in the world—as independent radio stations in South Korea begin to set up operation specifically to broadcast news into the DPRK.

It is well known that freedom of the press is absent in North Korea. According to one participant, "Journalists are press-ganged by the party into implementing a 'permanent information message,' which sets strict hierarchy for media work," namely, extolling the greatness of Kim Il Sung and Kim Jong Il, proclaiming the superiority of North Korean socialism, and denouncing imperialist and bourgeois corruption.

The prominent role of media was also discussed extensively as a means to provide truthful information to the North Korean populace. According to one participant, broadcast programs to North Korea include not only news and reports but also living testimonies, success stories of other communist countries, and dramas. Consensus was reached among participants that broadcasting is important to bring change from inside North Korea. According to one participant, history has shown that "silence has not led to progress"; change has come to authoritarian countries more smoothly where independent media were most active.

Currently, there are several independent radio stations based in Seoul that focus on reaching North Koreans with their broadcasts: Free North Korea Radio, Open Radio for North Korea, Radio Free Chosun, and Reform Radio. One of the innovative features of these stations is that they define themselves as the first independent media produced by North and

South Koreans for all Koreans. Media flow and radio programs were described as important; "if nothing else, North Koreans are at least able to hear a different message than the one their government puts out." This was said to be important for purposes of promoting critical thinking and so forth. This is the case because even well-intentioned education programs (e.g., English education) run by foreign embassies in Pyongyang for North Koreans are said to be at the mercy of the political regime.

One participant explained the efforts and the mission of media work as such: "One of the key lessons from the Eastern Europe experience is that you need to seek out and support programs for those people [defectors] that the North Korean regime hates and fears the most . . . If you don't, it's like throwing away a deck of cards if North Korean officials are used instead of defectors in the transition to unification. To avoid mistakes, do the homework on the rich set of lessons from the European experiences that suggest what was dysfunctional with these other states."

Yet the role of such independent media in South Korea is controversial, engaging much debate. Some participants questioned the effectiveness—and motives —of some of the radio stations' programming. Despite being supported by international donors, like other nongovernmental organizations (NGOs), some of these radio stations have operated—or still do—without ethical standards, pushing their own agenda. Therefore, it becomes even more imperative for human rights, North Korean defector, and media organizations to be equipped with capacity to operate clear missions and objectives with transparent operational guidelines and rules to raise the reputation of the organization. Such will eventually play a vital role in helping them to attract more funding and effectively utilize their potential for improving the human rights situation of North Koreans in the DPRK.

Economic Development, Participation, and Market Reform

Stable economic growth requires democracy. Economic freedom comes from political freedom. One participant explained the general relationship between economic development and democracy and emphasized how this relationship is strongly interconnected. Governance and institutions were said to be necessary for stable economic development: for example, transparency, accountability, anticorruption, participation, rule of law, private property rights protection, checks and balances, and freedom of information. The participant also stated that crony capitalism is not the entire market system, and competition and antimonopoly policy, contract enforcement, and a level playing field for business are necessary for the market system. He added that quality of development is equally important.

In this situation, the international community's engagement is closely tied with the lives of the North Korean people, in the most basic economic sense, which makes it more urgent and critical. One participant concluded that economic engagement with North Korea should be promoted on two levels: in the short term, it is necessary to provide humanitarian aid to improve the quality of life and dignity of North Korean people, which should not be influenced by political agendas; in the long term, there has to be a sustainable development plan to strengthen the country's economic capacity. It was believed that this improved economic capacity will bring reform and openness and improvement on human rights. Areas that strategies should target were said to be agriculture, energy, social infrastructure, information, science and technology, and tourism.

Another participant seconded the notion that the energy sector is a crucial sector to North Korea's economic development and emphasized the need for the international community to assist in the rebuilding of the DPRK energy infrastructure. Particularly, he pointed out that electricity and coal infrastructure problems feed back and link to problems throughout the economy. Both small and large-scale energy sector improvements were also believed to be "doable" and should not be contingent on improvements on democracy and human rights in the country. International assistance for internal policy and legal reforms to stimulate and sustain energy sector rebuilding in the DPRK would be needed—areas that possibly could be led by the international organizations that have interests in helping North Korea, such as IBRD, ADB, the UN, and specific nongovernmental organizations (NGOs), not just by the governments party to the six-party nuclear negotiations. The participant warned that the consequences of not addressing the energy sector problems sooner rather than later would be fatal; the vicious cycle of flooding, famine, and natural disasters from lack of energy and development would continue.

Many participants agreed that economic development is necessary in order to improve the human rights situation in North Korea and emphasized the importance of improving human rights and protecting the most basic and fundamental rights of North Korean residents. In order to do so, however, it was believed that humanitarian aid must be provided for first. Ultimately, a move in the direction toward development that is self-sufficient and sustainable could be made possible, as economic development is a goal shared by North Korea and the international community.

IV. Conclusion

North Korea's Road to Modernization

North Korea's Road to Modernization

There still exists a great divide between members of the governmental and nongovernmental communities (including scholars) on how best to go about improving the human rights situation in North Korea—can we work with the political regime to modernize the North, hoping that with economic development, improvement in human rights will follow; or do we work to crush it? The reality of this divide was never more evident in the discussion among conference and workshop participants, and a divide that is unlikely to be resolved itself. With this in mind, the writers of this report provide the following findings and suggestions:[36]

- Efforts should be made and conditions set up to encourage North Korea to pursue the road to modernization. In this regard, the experience of South Korea in the 1960s and 1970s, its authori-

---

36. This section was written exclusively by the North Korea Modernization Research Group of IFES. Participants neither reviewed nor approved this section, and therefore it should not be assumed that every participant subscribes to these findings and suggestions.

tarian government and export-oriented economic development strategies, should be more closely examined, as they may be a better fit to the North Korean context than other strategies. No country succeeded in incorporating development of both democracy and economy in the initial stages of industrialization. Rather, as the South Korean experience proves, industrialization even under authoritarian regimes can operate as a catalyst to the development of the foundation for the forces of democracy. Gradually but eventually, to achieve sustainable economic growth and development, North Korea will have to shed its authoritarian ways in favor of human rights norms and democracy.

- Economic development is necessary to improve the human rights situation in the DPRK; nevertheless, it should not trump the need to protect the most basic and fundamental rights of North Korean residents. Hence, while the conditions for promoting greater interaction and efforts to realize economic development in North Korea may not be present at this time, this should not stop the provision of humanitarian aid. Humanitarian aid must be provided for first, and at all times. Ultimately, a move in the direction toward development that is self-sufficient and sustainable could be made possible, as economic development is a goal shared by North Korea and the international community.

- Coordination among nongovernmental organizations (NGOs) working inside and outside North Korea seems a difficult prospect, as perspectives on the necessity of coordination diverge. While many see the value in "networking," the reality of working in an environment governed by an authoritarian regime means that coordination on the surface among nongovernmental organizations (NGOs) may jeopardize some of the meaningful humanitarian projects being done that actually reach the most vulnerable and intended recipients of aid.

- The possibility of taking a common approach to the problem of North Korea is improbable. Instead, the international community should work toward a common understanding of the situation in the DPRK, allowing for multiple, and hopefully complementary approaches. This appears the only way forward.

- Despite the apparent cleavages and stratification in North Korean society and the fracture in the relationship between the regime and populace, the current reality and character of the regime and atomized nature of society, along with the geopolitics of Northeast Asia (i.e., "the China's factor"), strongly negate the possibility of a regime collapse or the embrace of democracy in North Korea. Hence, political liberalization in the DPRK should be seen as a long-term goal.

- International donors should practice greater diligence before the decision is made to support a local nongovernmental organization (NGO) (i.e., South Korean NGO) claiming to promote North Korean human rights. Donors must be more cautious, examining more closely the local context in which a potential recipient for funding is operating to determine whether the organization's agenda and track record meet baseline ethical standards and codes of conduct.

- The North Korean defector community is a valuable resource that is only likely to grow in the future. Not only are "new settlers" valuable for promoting integration of future defectors into South Korean society, but they stand to be some of the most useful future practitioners and leaders of the peaceful unification process. In this regard, the nurturing of defectors' capacities, in particular through education of the youth among them, deserves more attention, from both the government and nongovernmental organizations (NGOs).
- It is important to recognize that change has come to authoritarian countries more smoothly where independent media were most active. Despite the apparent controversy, independent media (in particular radio stations) in South Korea that broadcast into North Korea can play a constructive role in bringing positive transformation from within the DPRK.
- Being equipped with the capacity to operate clear missions and objectives with transparent operational guidelines and codes of conduct is

absolutely crucial for any nongovernmental organization (NGO), but particularly those claiming to promote human rights. This is critical not only to safeguard the reputation of the community of nongovernmental organizations (NGOs) working for North Korean human rights as a whole but to help the community attract more funding in the future and to effectively utilize its potential for actually improving the human rights situation of North Koreans.

Bibliography

BOOKS

Cheong, Seong-Chang. "Kim Jong Il's Military-First Politics and a Change in the Power Elite." Paik, Haksoon and Seong-Chang Cheong, eds. *North Korea in Distress*. Seoul: The Sejong Institute, 2008.

Cho, Jeong-Ah, et al. *The Everyday Lives of North Koreans*. Seoul: KINU, 2009.

Haggard, Stephan and Marcus Noland. *Famine in North Korea*. New York: Columbia University Press, 2007.

Korean Institute for National Unification. *White Paper on Human Rights in North Korea*. Seoul: KINU, 2007.

Lankov, Andrei. *North of the DMZ*. London: McFarland & Co., 2007.

ARTICLES

"DPRK Food Prices Unstable as Lean Season Approaches." *NK Brief*. No. 10-04-28-1. April 28, 2010.

"DPRK Reopens Markets, Authorizes Food Sales." *NK Brief.* No. 10-2-24-1. February 24, 2010.

The Economist. *Country Report—North Korea.* November 2009.

"In North Korea, the Military Now Issues Economic Orders." *Washington Post*, November 3, 2009.

Institute for Far Eastern Studies. *NK Brief.* No. 10-3-3-1. March 3, 2010.

"Kim Jong Il's Sister Powers Up In North Korea." *Sydney Morning Herald.* February 18, 2010.

Kim, Sung-jin. "Actual Conditions of North Korean Defectors." *Vantage Point.* Vol. 31, No. 11. November 2008: 16–19.

Liang-Fenton, Debra. "Failing to Protect: Food Shortages and Prison Camps in North Korea." *Asian Perspective.* Vol. 31, No. 2 (Summer 2007): 47–74.

"N. Korean Parliament Boosts Kim Jong-il's Powers." *Chosun Ilbo.* September 25, 2009.

"North Korea Battles to Up Output in 150-day Campaign." *Reuters.* August 20, 2009.

"North Korea to Launch the New '100-day Battle.'" *NK Brief.* No. 09-15-1. September 15, 2009.

"North Korean Defectors: A Big Market for Matchmakers." *Time*. February 9, 2010.

"North Korean Food Shortages to Grow, Crimes of Necessity on the Rise." *NK Brief*. No. 09-11-02-1. November 2, 2009.

"North's Military Strengthens Its Grip." *JoongAng Ilbo*. April 21, 2009.

"Pyongyang Enacts Major Changes in Power Structure." *JoongAng Ilbo*. February 10, 2010.

Schuman, Michael. "The Real Crisis in North Korea? Food." *Time*. October 6, 2008.

ONLINE SOURCES

BBC. "North Korean Country Profile." Retrieved from http://news.bbc.co.uk/2/hi/country_profiles/1131421.stm#media.

Central Intelligence Agency. *The World Factbook*. Retrieved from https://www.cia.gov/library/publications/the-world-factbook/geos/kn.html#.

Feffer, John. "*Starting Where North Korea Is*." 38 North. Washington, D.C.: U.S.-Korea Institute at SAIS, Johns Hopkins University. May 1,

2010. Retrieved from http://www.38north.org/?p=529.

"Look at Little Sister." Posted on North Korean Leadership Watch. September 24, 2009. Retrieved from http://nkleadershipwatch.wordpress.com/.

Mansourov, Alexander. "North Korea: Changing but Stable." *Northeast Asia Peace and Security Network Policy Forum Online*. Nautilus Institution. May 12, 2010. Retrieved from http://www.nautilus.org/fora/security/10027/Mansourov.html.

"Mr. Jang and Mrs. Kim Go Global." North Korean Leadership Watch. February 11, 2010. Retrieved from http://nkleadershipwatch.wordpress.com/.

"North Korea Among the Worst Media on Earth." Daily NK. October 21, 2009. Retrieved from http://www.dailynk.com/english/read.php?cataId=nk00100&num=5555.

"North Korea's 2010 New Year's Joint Editorial" (English translation). Posted on Northeast Asian Matters. January 1, 2010. Retrieved February 10, 2010 from http://asiamatters.blogspot.com/2010/01/north-koreas-2010-

new-years-joint.html.

Reporters Without Borders. "Press Freedom Index 2008." Retrieved from http://en.rsf.org/press-freedom-index-2008,33.html.

U.S. Department of State. *2009 Human Rights Report: DPRK—Country Reports on Human Rights Practices.* Retrieved from www.state.gov/g/drl/rls/hrrpt/2009/eap/135995.htm.

Vorontsov, Alexander V. "North Korea's Military-First Policy: A Curse or a Blessing?" Brookings Institution. May 26, 2006. Retrieved from http://www.brookings.edu/opinions/2006/0526northkorea_vorontsov.aspx.

The Contributors

North Korea Modernization Research Group

Members of North Korea Modernization Research Group

Suhoon Lee (Director of IFES)

Kabwoo Koo (Professor, University of North Korean Studies)

Moonsoo Yang (Associate Professor, University of North Korean Studies)

Keunsik Kim (Associate Professor, Kyungnam University)

Soojung Lee (Assistant Professor, University of North Korean Studies)

Eulchul Lim (Research Professor, IFES)

Phillip H. Park (Associate Professor, Kyungnam University)

Dean Ouellette (Research Fellow, IFES)

Kelly Hur (Research Fellow, IFES)

Heekyung Son (Research Fellow, IFES)

Appendix

Appendix _ **117**

Map of the Korean Peninsula

Map of North Korea

Index

[A]
Agriculture
Aid
Air Force
Albania
Arduous March
ASEAN Regional Forum (ARF)
Asian Development Bank (ADB)
Authoritarianism
Autocracy

[B]
Black markets
British Broadcasting Corporation (BBC)
Broadcasts
Burma

[C]
Capacity building
Central Court
Central People's Committee
Changang
China, People's Republic of
Choego Inmin Hoeui,
    see Supreme People's Assembly
Chondoist Chongu Party

Civil security forces
Codes of conduct
Cold War
Communism
Communist legal theory
Communist Party,
    see Workers' Party of Korea
Constitution
Constitutional amendments
Corruption
Crony capitalism
Currency
Currency redenomination

[D] Defector
Defector-led nongovernmental organization (NGO)
Democracy
Democracy promotion
Democratic People's Republic of Korea (DPRK)
Denuclearization
Development
Development assistance
Dictatorship

Donor nations
Donor organizations
Donors
DPRK Socialist Constitution

[E] East Asian model
Eastern Europe
Economic adjustment measures,
  see July 1st economic measures
Economic development
Economic growth
Education
Effectiveness
Energy
Ethical standards
Exile community

[F] Famine
Food aid
Food and Agricultural Organization of the UN (FAO)
Food security
Food shortages
Food rationing

Foreign embassies
Freedom of expression
Freedom of information
Free North Korea Radio

[G]
General Assembly
Good governance
"Grand Bargain"
Gross National Income (GNI)
Ground forces

[H]
Hamgyong, North
Hamgyong, South
Hanawon
Health care
Human capital development
Human rights
Human rights abuses
Human rights documentation
Human rights organizations
Human rights situation
Humanitarian aid/assistance
Hwanghae, North
Hwanghae, South

[I]
Ideology
Independent media
Industrial Development Organization (IDO)
Industrialization
Infrastructure
Institute for Far Eastern Studies (IFES)
Integration
International aid
International Bank for Reconstruction and
    Development (IBRD)
International community
International Court of Justice (ICJ)
International donors
International School of Berne
International Telecommunications Satellite
    Organization (ITSO)
Inter-Parliamentary Union (IPU)
Investment
Ital jumin

[J]
Japan
Joson Inmingun (Korean People's Army Daily)
Juche
July 1st economic measures

[K] Kaesong Industrial Complex (KIC)
Kangsong taeguk
Kangwon
Kim Jong Il
Kim Jong Un
Kim Il Sung
Kim Kyong Hui
Kim Yong Dae
Kim Yong Il
Kim Yong Nam
Korea, North,
    see Democratic People's Republic of Korea
Korea, South, *see Republic of Korea*
Korea Institute for National Unification (KINU)
Korean Central Broadcasting Station
Korean Central News Agency (KCNA)
Korean Central TV
Korean People's Army (KPA)
Korean Workers' Party (KWP)
Kumgang Mountain tourism
Kyungnam University

[L]
Law
Leadership
Leadership structure
Leadership succession
Lee Myung-bak
Legal system
Liberalization
Life expectancy
Light industry

[M]
Malnutrition
Mansudae TV
Market
Market reform
Media
Military
Military-first, *see "Songun"*
Ministry of Trade, North Korean
Ministry of Unification, South Korean
Minju Choson (Democratic Korea)
Modernization

[N]   Naegak
Nason-si
National Defense Commission (NDC)
National Endowment for Democracy (NED)
Navy
Newspapers
Nuclear program
Nuclear test
Nuclear weapons
New settlers
New Year's Joint Editorial
Non-Aligned Movement (NAM)
Nongovernmental organizations (NGOs)
North Korean defector community
North Korean defectors
North Korean Human Rights Act
North Korea Modernization Research Team
North Korean People's Army

[O]   Open Radio for North Korea
Orascom

[P]
Park Bong Ju, Prime Minister
Park Nam Gi
Party Central Committee
Planned economy
Political liberalization
Politics
Poverty
Privatization
Public distribution system
Pyongan, North
Pyongan, South
Pyongyang
Pyongyang Times

[R]
Radio
Radio Free Chosun
Radio Free Europe
Radio Londres
Radio Marti
Reform
Reform Radio
Refugee
Reporters Without Borders

Republic of Korea (ROK)
Resettlement
Resettlement center
Reunification
Rodongja Sinmun (Workers' Newspaper)
Rodong Sinmun (Labor Daily)
Romania
Russia
Ryugyong Hotel

[S] Saeteomin
Science and technology
Self-reliance, *see Juche*
Six-Party Talks
Social Democratic Party
Sociocultural
Socioeconomic
Songbun
Songun
Special Rapporteur for Human Rights in the DPRK
Speed battle
Steel

Stratification
Suffrage
Supreme People's Assembly (SPA)

[T] *Talbukja*
Tourism
Trade
Training
Transparency

[U] Unification
Union of Soviet Socialist Republics (USSR)
United Nations (UN)
United Nations Conference on Trade and
 Development (UNCTAD)
United Nations Educational, Scientific,
 and Cultural Organization (UNESCO)
United Nations Resolutions
United Nations Sanctions
United States of America

[V] Vietnam
Voice of Korea

[W] Women
Worker's Party of Korea (WPK)
World Tourism Organization (UNWTO)

[Y] Yanggang
Youth